Easy Piano Pieces

Edited by Hugo Frey

Over 100 pieces by the masters of the symphony, ballet, and opera, plus Gilbert and Sullivan favorites and Christmas songs. Arranged for the beginning to intermediate grades.

T0085524

Cover photograph by David Zickl/SuperStock

Copyright © 1948 by Consolidated Music Publishers.
Published 1984 by Amsco Publications,
A Division of Music Sales Corporation, New York.

Order No. AM 41435
International Standard Book Number: 0.8256.4003.2

Exclusive Distributors:
Music Sales Corporation
257 Park Avenue South, New York, NY 10010 USA
Music Sales Limited
8/9 Frith Street, London W1V 5TZ England
Music Sales Pty. Limited
120 Rothschild Street, Rosebery, Sydney, NSW 2018, Australia

Printed in the United States of America by
Vicks Lithograph and Printing Corporation

Amsco Publications
New York/London/Sydney

Contents by Titles

When Broadcasting the compositions in this Book, give Performance Credit to CONSOLIDATED MUSIC PUBLISHERS, INC.

Contents by Composers

THE HAPPY FARMER

Arranged by
Hugo Frey

ROBERT SCHUMANN

DANCE OF THE SUGAR PLUM FAIRY

from "THE NUTCRACKER SUITE"

by PETER TSCHAIKOWSKY
Arranged by Hugo Frey

Moderately Slow *(Staccato)*

COUNTRY GARDENS

ENGLISH DANCE
Arranged by Hugo Frey

PETER AND THE WOLF

Arranged by
Hugo Frey

SERGEI PROKOFIEFF

Slow two beats

MOONLIGHT SONATA

Op. 27 No. 2 Abridged

Arranged by
James Palmeri

LUDWIG van BEETHOVEN

JEANIE WITH THE LIGHT BROWN HAIR

Arranged by
James Palmeri

STEPHEN C. FOSTER

THE HAREBELL

William Smallwood

THE COWSLIP

WILLIAM SMALLWOOD

DOLORES

Op. 170

Arranged by
James Palmeri

EMILE WALDTEUFEL

Grazioso

WALTZ OF THE FLOWERS

from the "NUTCRACKER SUITE"

Arranged by
James Palmeri

PETER TSCHAIKOWSKY

Tempo di Valse

H. M. S. PINAFORE

SELECTION

Arranged by
James Palmeri

SIR ARTHUR SULLIVAN

Allegro   *We Sail The Ocean Blue*

Moderato

Allegretto   *I'm Called Little Buttercup*

Andante *Sorry Her Lot*

Marziale   *I Am The Monarch Of The Sea*

ANVIL CHORUS

from "IL TROVATORE"

Arranged by
P. Ballatore

GIUSEPPE VERDI

Moderato (♩ = 112)

ON THE BEAUTIFUL BLUE DANUBE

*Arranged by
James Palmeri*

JOHANN STRAUSS

Intro.
Tempo di Valse

OH! SUSANNA

Arranged by
P. Ballatore

STEPHEN C. FOSTER

BEAUTIFUL DREAMER

Arranged by
P. Ballatore

STEPHEN C. FOSTER

CHOPIN MEDLEY

*Arranged by
James Palmeri*

FREDERIC CHOPIN

Valse, Op. 70, No. 1

Allegro Moderato

Tempo di Valse

Lento

Valse, Op. 34, No. 2

Valse lente

Minute Waltz, Op. 64, No. 1

Tempo di Valse

Moderato

Polonaise, Op. 53

THE STAR-SPANGLED BANNER

Arranged by
P. Ballatore

FRANCIS SCOTT KEY
JOHN STAFFORD SMITH

COLUMBIA, THE GEM OF THE OCEAN

Arranged by
P. Ballatore

TRADITIONAL

CHRISTMAS MEDLEY

MERRY CHIMES

Arranged by
BYRON C. TAPLEY

ROSES FROM THE SOUTH

Arranged by
James Palmeri

JOHANN STRAUSS

Theme from

CONCERTO No. 1

Arranged by
P. Ballatore

PETER TSCHAIKOWSKY

Allegro maestoso

BARCAROLLE

from "TALES OF HOFFMANN"

J. OFFENBACH

Arranged by
Byron C. Tapley

THE SKATERS WALTZ

Op. 183

Arranged by
James Palmeri

EMIL WALDTEUFEL

Intro.
Tempo di Valse

Waltz

THE WASHINGTON POST

MARCH

Arranged by
Hugo Frey

JOHN PHILIP SOUSA

Lively March tempo

G# and Ab are alike.

Trio

TWO GUITARS

Arranged by
P. Ballatore

TRADITIONAL

Moderato

Andante

SERENADE FOR STRINGS

WALTZ

*Transcription by
Hugo Frey*

PETER TSCHAIKOWSKY

SERENADE

PUNCHINELLO

Arranged by
P. Ballatore

R. DRIGO

BERCEUSE

from "JOCELYN"

Arranged by
Byron C. Tapley

BENJAMIN GODARD

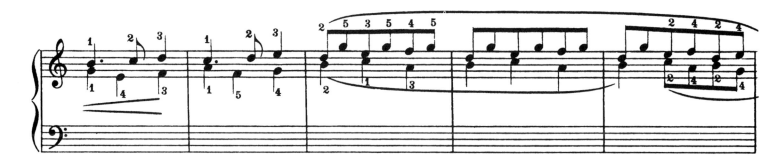

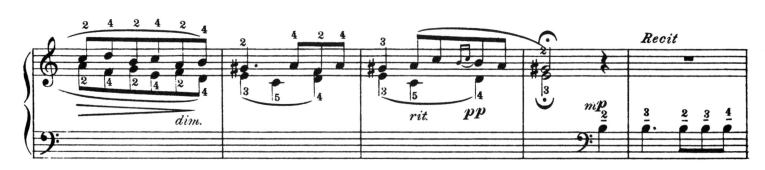

LILY

Op. 160, No. 6

H. LICHNER

Tempo di Polacca

LITTLE FAIRY WALTZ

L. STREABBOG

SOUVENIR

Arranged by
Byron C. Tapley

FRANZ DRDLA

Andante

CARMEN

SELECTION

Edited by
J. Frank Leve

GEORGES BIZET

Allegro moderato   *March of the Toreadors*

Allegretto quasi Andantino   *Habanera*

Moderato

The Sound of Triangles

Toreador Song

AIDA

SELECTION

Edited by
J. Frank Leve

GIUSEPPE VERDI

Tempo di marcia   *Glory To Isis*

Andantino *Heav'nly Aida*
with expression

Tempo di marcia *Grand March*

ELEGIE

Arranged by
Byron C. Tapley

JULES MASSENET

TRAUMEREI

Arranged by
Byron C. Tapley

ROBERT SCHUMANN

NARCISSUS

Op. 13, No. 4

Gracefully, with moderate tempo

ETHELBERT NEVIN
Arranged by Hugo Frey

Tempo primo

ANDANTINO

ARAM KHACHATURIAN

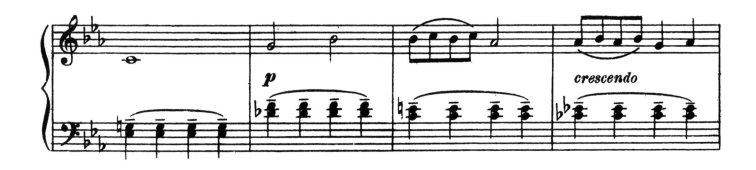

SALUT D'AMOUR

LOVE'S GREETING

*Arranged by
Byron C. Tapley*

EDWARD ELGAR

GOOD BYE

Arranged by
Byron C. Tapley

F. PAOLO TOSTI

Adagio

SEXTETTE

from "LUCIA DI LAMMERMOOR"

Arranged by
Byron C. Tapley

G. DONIZETTI

OVER THE WAVES

*Arranged by
Byron C. Tapley*

JUVENTINO ROSAS

LIGHT CAVALRY OVERTURE

Arranged by
Byron C. Tapley

F. von SUPPE

SONG OF INDIA

Arranged by
Byron C. Tapley

N. RIMSKY-KORSAKOFF

MARCH

from "RAYMOND"

Arranged by
Byron C. Tapley

AMBROISE THOMAS

Allegro

AH, I HAVE SIGHED TO REST ME

from "IL TROVATORE"

GIUSEPPE VERDI

Arranged by
A. H. Rosewig

Andante

DANUBE WAVES

JAN IVANOVICI

Arranged by
Byron C. Tapley

PRELUDE IN C# MINOR

SERGEI RACHMANINOFF

Arranged by
Byron C. Tapley

HUNGARIAN DANCE No. 5

JOHANNES BRAHMS

Arranged by
P. Ballatore

Allegretto moderato

PILGRIMS' CHORUS

from "TANNHAUSER"

Arranged by
Byron C. Tapley

RICHARD WAGNER

THE DYING POET

Arranged by
Byron C. Tapley

LOUIS M. GOTTSCHALK

CIRIBIRIBIN

Arranged by
Byron C. Tapley

A. PESTALOZZA

SERENATA

Arranged by
Byron C. Tapley

M. MOSZKOWSKI

WEDDING MARCHES

*Arranged by
Byron C. Tapley*

WAGNER-MENDELSSOHN

Alla Marcia *Bridal Chorus from "Lohengrin"—Wagner*

Wedding March—Mendelssohn

ROMANCE

ROBERT SCHUMANN

EVENING STAR

from "TANNHAUSER"

Arranged by
Byron C. Tapley

RICHARD WAGNER

Andante

MOMENT MUSICALE

Op. 94—No. 3

FRANZ SCHUBERT

MINUET

from "DON JUAN"

WOLFGANG MOZART

UNFINISHED SYMPHONY

THEME

FRANZ SCHUBERT

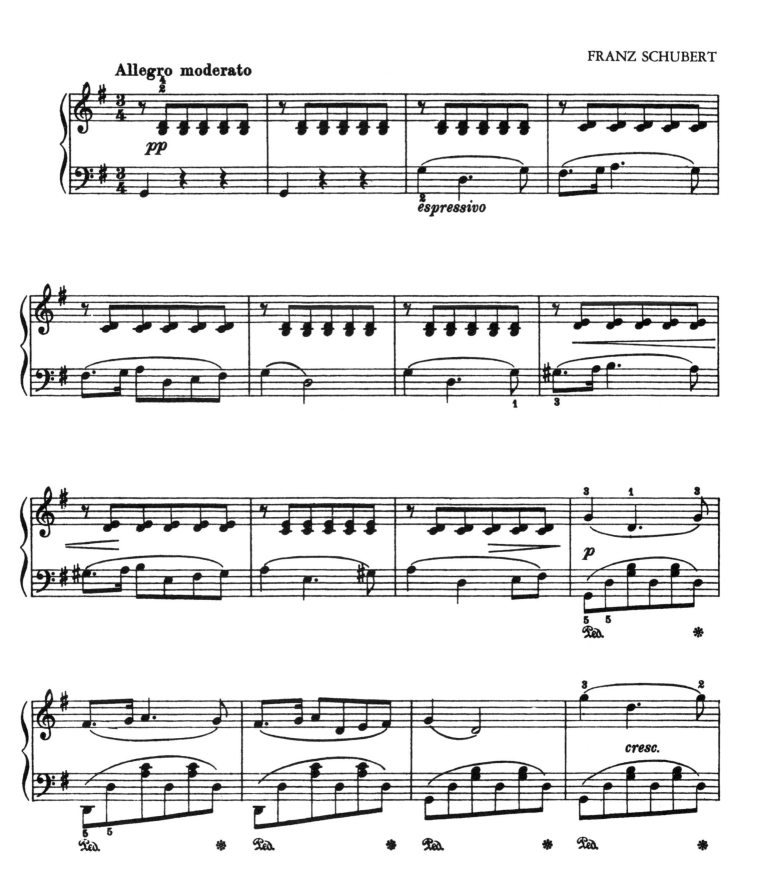

CONCERTO

Op. 18—THEMES

Transcription by
Hugo Frey

SERGEI RACHMANINOFF

(1st Theme)
Moderato

(2nd Theme)
Moderately slow

ANGEL'S SERENADE

Arranged by
A. H. Rosewig

G. BRAGA

MARCH OF THE DWARFS

Op. 54, No. 3

EDVARD GRIEG

ESTUDIANTINA

WALTZES

Arranged by
James Palmeri

EMILE WALDTEUFEL

LA GOLONDRINA

THE SWALLOW

N. SERRADELL

EMPEROR WALTZ

JOHANN STRAUSS

MEXICAN HAT DANCE

TRADITIONAL

Theme from

RED POPPY BALLET

R. GLIERE

FLOWER SONG

GUSTAV LANGE

Arranged by
W. A. Phillips

Lento

a little faster

dim

molto rit.

molto
rit.

D.S. al fine

THE IRISH WASHERWOMAN

JIG

TRADITIONAL

HIGHLAND FLING

TRADITIONAL

SAILOR'S HORNPIPE

TRADITIONAL

GARRY OWEN

JIG

TRADITIONAL

SPINNING SONG

Op. 14 No. 4

Edited by
J. Frank Leve

ALBERT ELLMENREICH

LES DEMONS S'AMUSENT

VLADIMIR REBIKOFF

ON WINGS OF SONG

FELIX MENDELSSOHN

SABER DANCE

from "GAYNE BALLET"

Transcription by
Hugo Frey

ARAM KHACHATURIAN

Left hand may be simplified thus:

THE KALENDER PRINCE

from "SCHEHEREZADE"

N. RIMSKY-KORSAKOFF

CUCKOO WALTZ

J. E. JONASSON
Arranged by William C. Schoenfeld

Moderate Waltz tempo

RUSTIC DANCE

Simplified by Hugo Frey

C. R. HOWELL

Moderately bright tempo

THE MERRY WIDOW WALTZ

FRANZ LEHAR

Valse

con molto sentimento

ANDANTINO

EDWIN H. LEMARE

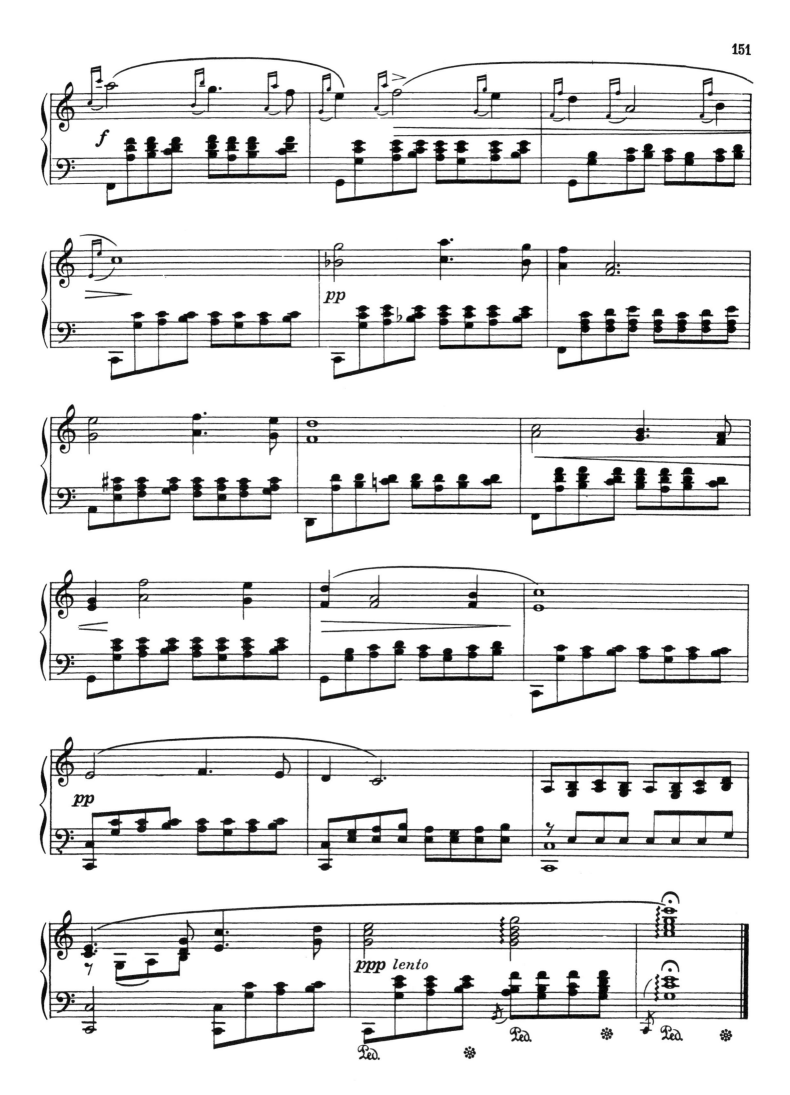

THE BLACK HAWK WALTZ

MARY E. WALSH

MENUET

Op. 14 No. 1

IGNAZ J. PADEREWSKI

Allegretto